Published by
Arcturus Publishing Limited

ISBN 1-84193-084-9

This edition published 2001

Printed and bound in Italy

Inner typography and layout by Alex Ingr
& Zeta Fitzpatrick, Moo Design

Cover design by Susi Martin

Editor: Anne Fennell

© Arcturus Publishing Limited
1-7 Shand Street, London SE1 2ES

Knock, Knock...

Who's there?

Double Glazing Salesman
.....hello.....hello...

Knock, Knock...

Who's there?

Pete

Pete who?

Pete after me, 'I am going
to open the door now...'

KNOCK KNOCK

Knock, Knock...
Who's there?
Geoff
Geoff who?
Geoff to ask that question every single day?

Knock, Knock...
Who's there?
June
June who?
June know how long I've been waiting out here?

4

Knock, Knock...

Who's there ?

Can you Linda

Can you Linda who ?

Can you Linda me a cup of sugar ?

Knock, Knock...

Who's there ?

Ronnie

RONNIE who ?

**Ronnie nose – need a hanky –
let me in – quick !**

KNOCK KNOCK

Knock, Knock...

Who's there?

Deb

Deb who?

Deb better be a good reason for keeping me waiting out here!

Knock, Knock...

Who's there?

Eileen Dover

Eileen Dover who?

Eileen Dover your fence and broke it!

KNOCK KNOCK

Knock, Knock...
who's there ?
Sandy
sandy who ?
Sandy you living next door innit ?!

Knock Knock...
who's there ?
Herbert...
Herbert who ?
Herbert you come to the door and see for yourself ?!

KNOCK KNOCK

Knock, Knock...
Who's there ?
Vera
Vera Who ?
Vera long way from home
and need a map !

Knock, Knock...
Who's there ?
Paul
Paul Who ?
Paul the other one it's got bells on !

Knock, Knock...
who's there ?
Atish
atish who ?
Bless You !

SIGH..

Knock, Knock...
who's there ?
Moore
Moore who ?
Moore or less the same person as before !

KNOCK KNOCK

Knock, Knock...

Who's there?

Toulouse

Toulouse who?

Toulouse are better than one in a busy house I always say !

Knock, Knock...

Who's there?

Germaine

Germaine who?

Germaine I can't come in unless I tell you ?

Knock, Knock...

Who's there?

Tamara

Tamara who?

Tamara's my birthday, Don't forget !

Knock, Knock...

Who's there?

Harmony

Harmony who?

Harmony times do I have to tell you ?!

Knock Knock...

Who's there?

Atilla...

atilla who?

Atilla you open dis door I'm a gonna stand here !

KNOCK KNOCK

Knock, Knock...
who's there ?
Dan
Dan who ?
Dan Dan Dan Dan Daaaannnn !

Knock, Knock...
who's there ?
Don
Don who ?
Don be afraid....look into
my eyes... you are feeling sleepy...

Knock, Knock...

Who's there ?

A guest

a guest who ?

A guest you wouldn't recognise my voice !

Knock, Knock...

Who's there ?

Carrie

Carrie who ?

Carrie on like this and I'll freeze to death out here !

Knock, Knock...
Who's there ?
France
France who ?
France y meeting you here !

Knock, Knock...
Who's there ?
Adolf
Adolf who ?
Adolf ball hit me in de mouf !

Knock, Knock...
who's there?
Iona
Iona who?
Iona have eyes for you!

Knock, Knock...
who's there?
Chris
Chris who?
Chris Packet, but
my friends call me
Russell!

Knock, Knock...
Who's there ?
Justin
Justin who ?
Just in time to open the door for me !

Knock, Knock...
Who's there ?
Lettuce
Lettuce who ?
Lettuce in and you'll find out !

Knock, Knock...
Who's there ?
Mandy
Mandy who ?
Mandy lifeboats !

Knock, Knock...
Who's there ?
Ivor
Ivor Who ?
Ivor message for a Mr Smith ?!

Knock, Knock...
Who's there ?
Shirley
Shirley who ?
Shirley you know the sound of my voice by now ?

Knock, Knock...

Who's there?

Noah

Noah who?

Noah a good place to hide from this rain?

Knock, Knock...

Who's there?

Wooden shoe

Wooden shoe who?

Wooden shoe like to see?

Knock, Knock...
Who's there?
Jester
Jester Who?
Jester minute I've forgotten!

Knock, Knock...
Who's there?
May-Belle
May-Belle Who?
May-Belle don't work either,
so I'm knocking!

Knock, Knock...
Who's there?
Kent...
KENT Who?
Kent you fix the doorbell?

Knock Knock...
Who's there?
Dismay...
Dismay Who?
**Dismay be the last time
I come round here!**

Knock Knock...
Who's there?
Twitter...
Twitter who?
You got an owl in there?

Knock Knock...
Who's there?
Snow...
Snow who?
Snow joke being out here
in the cold, let me in!
Knock Knock...

Knock Knock...
Who's there?
Nona...
Nona Who?
Nona your business!

Knock Knock...
Who's there?
Luke...
Luke Who?
Luke, stop messing about and let me in!

Knock Knock...
Who's there ?
Police...
Police who ?
Police let me in, I'm freezing out here !

Knock Knock...
Who's there ?
Pat...
Pat who ?
Actually it's Steve, I was just doing an impersonation of Pat !

Knock Knock...

who's there ?

Phil...

Phil who ?

**Phil this bag with money,
I'm a burglar !**

Knock Knock...

who's there ?

Guess...

Guess who ?

**Hang on, haven't we got this
mixed up somehow ?**

KNOCK KNOCK

Knock Knock...
Who's there?
Boo...
Boo who?
No need to get upset,
it's only a game!

Knock Knock...
Who's there?
The man from next door...
The man from next door who?
The man from next door who has
clearly come home to the wrong
house, sorry!

Knock Knock...
Who's there?
Dennis...
Dennis who?
Dennis must be the right place –
he said you'd ask that!

Knock Knock...
who's there?
Ivan...
Ivan Who?
Ivan to come in –
open the door!

Knock Knock...
who's there?
The Spice Girls...
Come in, come in, how rude of me
to keep you waiting...

Knock Knock...
Who's there ?
Jeanie...
Jeanie Who ?
**Jeanie comprend pas –
je suis Francais !**

Knock Knock...
Who's there ?
Ivor...
Ivor Who ?
Ivor key of my own now !

Knock Knock...
Who's there ?
Bill...
Bill who ?
Bill-ieve it or not this is a joke !

Knock Knock...
Who's there ?
Frank...
Frank who ?
Frankenstein !

Knock Knock...

who's there ?

Bert...

Bert who ?

Bert surely you recognise my voice !

Knock Knock...

who's there ?

Geezer...

Geezer who ?

Geezer couple of minutes and I'll pick this lock !

KNOCK KNOCK

Knock Knock...
who's there ?
Tim...
Tim Who ?
T-I-M-B-E-R !@*!!

Knock Knock...
who's there ?
L.E....
L.E. Who ?
L.E. Funt !

Knock Knock...
who's there ?
Kipper...
kipper who ?
Kipper your hands off my ice cream !

Knock Knock...
who's there ?
Snow...
snow who ?
**Snow use – I can't remember.
Knock Knock...**

KNOCK KNOCK

Who's there?
Ivor...
Ivor who?
Ivor got my fingers stuck
in your letter flap !

Knock Knock...
Who's there?
Howill...
Howill who?
**Howill you have your egg –
fried, boiled or scrambled ?**

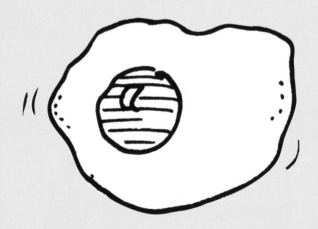